THE AUDUBON SOCIETY POCKET GUIDES

A Chanticleer Press Edition

Sidney Horenstein
American Museum of Natural History
Department of Invertebrates

FAMILIAR FOSSILS

Alfred A. Knopf, New York

This is a Borzoi Book
Published by Alfred A. Knopf, Inc.

Prepared and produced by Chanticleer Press, Inc.,
New York.
Color reproductions by Reprocolor International s.r.l.,
Milan, Italy.
Typeset by Dix Type Inc., Syracuse, New York.
Printed and bound by Dai Nippon, Tokyo, Japan.

First Printing.

Library of Congress Catalog Number: 87-46018
ISBN: 0-394-75791-2

Contents

How to Use This Guide

Fossils are a fascinating but often overlooked part of the natural world around us. They can be found nearly everywhere, and knowing something about them gives us glimpse of the landscapes and often strange living things that existed millions of years ago.

Coverage
This guide illustrates and describes 80 of the most abundant and striking fossils found in North America, representing 12 basic groups of plants and animals.

Organization
This easy-to-use pocket guide is divided into three parts: introductory essays and a geological time chart; illustrated accounts of the fossils; and appendices.

Introduction
As a basic introduction, the essay "What Is a Fossil?" examines the nature of fossils and how they are formed and preserved. "Fossils and Time" explains how the immense span of geological time has been measured, dated, and divided into eons, eras, periods, and epochs, each with its own name. This is followed by a graphic presentation of the time scale itself to help you understand the geological periods used in this guide. "Fossil Groups" describes the 12 major groups in the guide and places them in their geological context. The essay "Collecting Fossils" gives you tips on how to find fossils and how to preserve them

once you have removed them from the rocks in which they are found.

The Fossils   This section includes 80 color plates, arranged visually by shape and overall appearance. All of the major groups of fossils are represented except reptiles, amphibians, birds, and mammals. Each of these fossils is a genus—a group of closely related species that may have lived for a very long period of time. Some of the fossils in this book still survive as living animals or plants today. Facing each color plate is a description of the important field marks of the fossil, an indication of the geological period or periods when it lived in North America, and a brief statement of where in North America it occurs. An introductory paragraph provides additional facts about each fossil creature's habits or history. For quick reference, a drawing indicates the major group to which the fossil belongs.

Appendices   A glossary defines terms that are commonly used in the study of fossils. Following the glossary is an index.

Most parts of the country have fossil-bearing rocks. This guide is intended to help you to discover, identify, and enjoy the fossils that are common in your area.

What Is a Fossil?

The word fossil refers to the remains or traces of ancient living things. For a plant or animal to become a fossil it has to be buried and preserved in sediments, safe from forces that would destroy it if it were left exposed on the surface.

Age

The oldest known fossils are algae—one-celled plants—about 3.5 billion years old. The well-known trilobites are found in rocks that are hundreds of millions of years old. Fossils are also found in rock, sand, or clay that may be only tens of millions, or hundreds of thousands, of years old. Just how old must a plant or animal be to be called a fossil? One rule of thumb, used in this book, is that if the animal or plant lived more than 11,000 years ago, it is a fossil. But for some scientists, the remains of creatures that became extinct only 50 or 100 years ago are also fossils.

Fossil Traces

Not only are the actual remains of animals and plants fossils, but so are any traces they have left behind. As animals move across the sea floor, they may leave tracks or trails on the mud. These impressions may be preserved in the rocks. Worms burrowing through loose sediments often leave a tube, which may become filled with fine silt after the worm is gone. Plants such as grasses may bend over and sway in the breeze and leave grooves in the sand. The sap of trees may dry up and be preserved as amber. Petroleum and natural gas are products of the decay of living things, and are called fossil fuels.

Most fossils clearly look like plants or animals. Some are preserved intact, but most are only fragments of the ancient plant or animal. Usually just the hard parts or skeletons survive as fossils; only rarely are the soft parts of organisms preserved.

Chemical Changes
Over the ages, most fossils are altered chemically. The original crystal structure of the fossil may change, without a gain or loss of material. Or the original material may be replaced by another substance. In soft-bodied plants and animals, gases like oxygen, hydrogen, and nitrogen may evaporate as the organism decays, leaving only a film of carbon. A skeleton may be dissolved away by water, leaving a cavity called a mold in the sediment. The surface of the cavity bears the impression of the organism. Often the mold is then filled with new material and the filling is called a cast. Fossils are commonly found as casts or molds, without any of the original organic material left.

Fossils and Time

When you show your fossil collection to friends, you will probably tell them that the specimens are tens or hundreds of millions of years old. Your friends will almost certainly ask you how you know this. You must then give them a short course in geological time.

Relative Time

Sedimentary rocks, the kinds that contain fossils, are deposited one layer on top of another. The lowest layers formed first and are the oldest, the next layer up is younger, and so on until the uppermost layer, which is the youngest of all. Comparing fossils, early geologists used this principle to match the sequence of rocks in one area with that in another. Eventually, after correlating countless sequences and their fossils, a worldwide time scale was constructed, and standard names like Cambrian, Silurian, and Cretaceous were given to the different divisions of time. But although this principle, worked out about 200 years ago, tells us the relative ages of rocks, it cannot tell us their absolute age—how old they are in years.

Absolute Time

It was not until the end of the 19th century, with the discovery of radioactivity, that absolute ages in years could be assigned to the geological time scale. A radioactive element such as strontium or uranium breaks down at a known rate, changing to a different isotope of the same element or to another element. By knowing how much of the original element is still in a rock and how much has been replaced by a new isotope or element, we can determine the absolute age of the rock. This method can be used only with igneous rocks, those that were once molten. To determine the age of sedimentary rocks—the ones that contain fossils—we must find places where sedimentary rocks have been invaded by igneous rocks. We know only that the igneous rock must be more recent than the layers it has pierced. But after correlating thousands of such cases, geologists have assigned absolute ages to the relative time scale.

Divisions of Time The largest divisions of the time scale are the Precambrian and Phanerozoic eons. Fossils are not abundant in ancient Precambrian rocks, although this eon represents about 80 percent of geological time. The Phanerozoic, the eon of abundant life, is divided into three major eras: Paleozoic (Ancient Life), Mesozoic (Middle Life), and Cenozoic (Recent Life). The ends of the Paleozoic and Mesozoic eras were marked by major crises in which many animals became extinct. Eras are further divided into periods, and periods into epochs.

11

Geological Time Scale

4,600 to 570 million years ago	Precambrian Eon
570	Phanerozoic Eon
500	
430	
395	
345	
325	
280	
225	
190	
136	
65	
54	
37.5	
26	
5	
1.8	
11 thousand years ago to present	

Paleozoic Era	Cambrian Period	
	Ordovician Period	
	Silurian Period	
	Devonian Period	
	Mississippian Period	
	Pennsylvanian Period	
	Permian Period	
Mesozoic Era	Triassic Period	
	Jurassic Period	
	Cretaceous Period	
Cenozoic Era	Tertiary Period	Paleocene Epoch
		Eocene Epoch
		Oligocene Epoch
		Miocene Epoch
		Pliocene Epoch
	Quarternary Period	Pleistocene Epoch
		Recent Epoch

Fossil Groups

The fossils in this guide belong to 12 major groups. The most important features of each of these groups are noted here. Many of these groups still exist today.

Arthropods
Animals with a hard outer skeleton, a segmented body, and jointed appendages, the arthropods include the trilobites, *Eurypterus*, and insects, crabs, and spiders.

Bivalves
These are mollusks with two platelike valves or shells— one on each side of the soft body within. Only the shells usually survive as fossils.

Brachiopods
Like the bivalves, these animals have two shells enclosing the body, but they are oriented on top and bottom, not on the sides. Only the shells usually survive as fossils.

Bryozoans
Very small, tentacled creatures, bryozoans live in colonies. They resemble some corals but do not have partitions in the cavity containing each animal.

Cephalopods
Fossil cephalopods were mollusks with a coiled or straight, chambered shell; the chamber walls appear as lines or sutures outside the shell. Octopuses and squids are modern cephalopods without an outer shell.

Corals
Most corals are tiny animals that live in colonies. They

14

form a stony skeleton with a cavity for each individual coral; the cavity usually contains thin partitions.

Echinoderms A group that includes sea urchins, crinoids, and blastoids, most echinoderms have a hard, five-part, circular outer skeleton that often bears spines.

Gastropods Snails and most other gastropods are soft-bodied animals with a coiled shell that has an opening called an aperture through which the animal extends.

Graptolites Living in colonies, these animals formed tubes that were often branched. These fossils are very distantly related to vertebrates, including humans.

Plants Fossil plants include trees, ferns and their relatives, and marine algae. The most commonly preserved plant remains are impressions of leaves and bark.

Sponges Round or vase-shaped, sponges are simple animals with an inside cavity that communicates with the outside through pores and other openings.

Tentaculitids These common fossils consisted of simple hollow tubes. It is not known what kind of animals they were.

Arthropods
Cambrian to Recent
pages 162–178

Bivalves
Early Cambrian to Recent
pages 106; 118–128

Brachiopods
Early Cambrian to Recent
pages 130–160

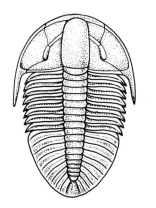

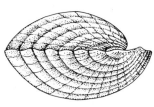

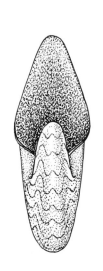

Echinoderms
Early Cambrian to Recent
pages 70–78

Gastropods
Cambrian to Recent
pages 88–104, 108

Graptolites
Cambrian to Mississippian
pages 180–182

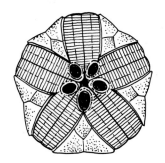

Plants
Precambrian to Recent
pages 24–36

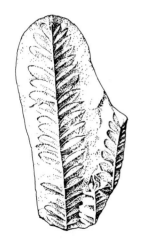

Sponges
Precambrian to Recent
pages 64–68

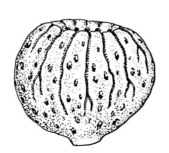

Tentaculitids
Early Silurian to Late Devonian
page 80

Collecting Fossils

About 70 percent of the land is covered with limestone, sandstone, or shale—the sedimentary rocks that contain fossils. Metamorphic rocks, those changed by heat and pressure, very rarely contain fossils. The third type of rocks, igneous rocks, were once molten and therefore lack fossils. Some fossils are not found in rocks at all, but in loose sand, gravel, or clay.

Tools

The rock your fossils are preserved in will determine the tools you need. If you live in an area where the rock is hard, you will need a mason's hammer with a chisel end, and a second hammer for hitting the first to split the rock along the layers. Some collectors also use a hammer with long chisels to pry rock away from outcrops. Small chisels are useful for delicate work—separating fossils from the rock around them. Use a shovel to dig fossils out of loose sand or gravel, and sieves with different mesh sizes will help to separate fossils from sand. Don't overlook the very small ones.

In the Field

Once you have collected your fossils, you will want to get them home safely. Write a label for each fossil, listing the date and where you collected it, the rock layer that contained it, and anything else you observe about the rocks. This information makes your fossils scientifically valuable, and must be recorded on the spot. Tape the label to the specimen. Your fossils should then be wrapped carefully in newspapers. Small vials or plastic boxes are good for tiny fossils. Then place your finds in a sturdy bag.

At Home   Once you are home, catalog and number the fossils. The catalog—a book or card file—should contain all the information you noted in the field. The fossils may need cleaning. An old toothbrush is a good tool for removing loose grains, and for harder materials, dental picks are excellent. Dentists are often willing to give you instruments that are worn out.

Where to Look   At first you may have difficulty finding collecting areas. If there is a fossil club or a rock and mineral club in your area, its members may be very knowledgeable about collecting places. Other sources of information are university geology departments and state geological surveys.

A Last Word   Familiarize yourself with any state laws that govern the collecting of fossils. Many outcrops are on private property; get permission before you collect. Finally, take only what you really want, and leave something for others; almost all outcrops are limited.

THE FOSSILS

Alethopteris

During the Pennsylvanian Period, *Alethopteris* and other plants called seed ferns flourished in and around swamps. When they died, they sank to the bottom where stagnant water slowed the rate of decay. Such an accumulation of slowly decomposing plant material is called peat. As peat beds are buried under sand and mud, the resulting rise in pressure and temperature compresses the peat and begins to change it into coal. In higher grades of coal, the structure of the plant material is no longer recognizable. Today *Alethopteris* and other seed ferns form the coal beds in the eastern United States.

Identification 3–4″. Fronds long, with many long, bladelike leaflets that have wide bases and wide round tops. Ribs and veins usually visible.

Age Pennsylvanian.

Range Widespread in North America.

Annularia

If you want to get a good idea of how *Annularia* looked, find a living horsetail (*Equisetum*), which often grows in poor or disturbed soil. *Annularia* is the name given leaves that grew on trees called *Calamites*. Although it is now known that both names refer to the same plant, the two names are still used for convenience. The leaves look like rosettes arranged along a thick string. Some scientists think that the flattened appearance of the leaves is due to compression during fossilization, but others think the leaves were oriented that way in life to receive a maximum amount of light.

Identification 3″. Foliage arranged in circles of 8–32 narrow, lance-shaped leaves at evenly spaced joints on stems and branches.

Age Mississippian to Pennsylvanian.

Range Widespread in North America.

Neuropteris

This striking, fernlike fossil is commonly found in the waste piles adjacent to coal mines or pits. Ferns reproduce by spores, but *Neuropteris* reproduced by seeds and was one of the seed ferns. Some seed ferns grew to a height of 70 feet and a diameter of 2 feet. Many specimens of *Neuropteris* have been found with the seeds attached. In some, the seeds are at the tip of the frond, and in others they are along the midrib, each seed replacing a leaflet. These were plants of warm climates, so when their fossils are found in cool regions, this tells us these places were once warmer than they are now.

Identification 4″. Fronds composed of many alternate, oval leaflets attached to stems at a single point. Larger leaflets may be lobed at bases. Veins and midrib distinct.

Age Pennsylvanian.

Range Widespread in North America.

Ginkgo

Common today on many city streets, trees in the Ginkgo family evolved near the end of the Paleozoic Era, were widespread by the Jurassic Period, and then declined during the Tertiary. They grew in the western United States until the Miocene Epoch and then disappeared. The modern tree was unknown in the western world until the 17th century, when it was discovered in cultivation in Japan and China. In 1956 *Ginkgo biloba* was discovered growing in the wild in China. It is the only modern species, and is often cited as an example of a living fossil.

Identification 2″. Leaves fan-shaped, unlobed to deeply lobed. Veins nearly parallel and dividing often. Living leaves feel leathery. Male and female cones on separate trees. Leaves deciduous.

Age Jurassic to Recent.

Range Western North America.

Calamites

This tree formed dense jungles in swamps during the coal age and grew as tall as 65 feet, with creeping underground stems. *Calamites* is the name given to the stems and trunk of the tree, while *Annularia* is the name used for the leaves. Most fossils of *Calamites* are casts of the interior of a trunk. While the tree was still alive its interior rotted away, and when the tree died and fell into the swamp, the space was filled with mud. The hardened mud inside formed the cast.

Identification   Trunk with distinct nodes or raised riblike rings regularly spaced with parallel, vertical ribs between them. Leaves (2–12″) or branches attached in circles at nodes. Branch scars much larger than leaf scars.

Age   Mississippian to Permian.

Range   Widespread in North America.

Lepidodendron

This striking tree grew to 100 feet tall and 3 feet in diameter in freshwater or brackish swamps. The root system of *Lepidodendron* was long; one root was traced for 39 feet through ancient swamp sediments. *Lepidodendron* and related plants were abundant in the coal age—the Mississippian and Pennsylvanian periods. The living club mosses (*Lycopodium*) are related to *Lepidodendron*. Both reproduce by spores.

Identification Size variable. Trunk has diamond-shaped leaf cushions where leaf was attached; prominent scars in upper part of each diamond. Center of scar with 3 tiny circles marking location of vessels between leaf and stems.

Age Mississippian to Permian.

Range Widespread in North America.

Receptaculites

Until about 20 years ago, these attractive spiral-patterned plant fossils were thought to be sponges. Study of the fossils revealed them to be algae that secreted calcium carbonate that was preserved. *Receptaculites* lived near coral reefs, but usually not on the reef itself. When found on a reef, it often grew wedged in between animals, such as corals. *Receptaculites* preferred quiet water and seems to have thrived in water 20 feet deep. When these fossils are found in muddy sediments, they are often the only ones there.

Identification   A globular or platter-shaped mass up to 1' in diameter. Surface with rectangular plates arranged in clockwise and counterclockwise spirals, like seeds in a sunflower. Plates connected to one another by pillars.

Age   Ordovician to Devonian.

Range   Most common in Midwest.

Favosites

During the Silurian Period and much of the Devonian, this coral was one of the most important reef builders, found in limestones in warm, tropical lagoons. Many species have been described based on small variations in the individual animals, called corallites. The distinctive growth form of *Favosites* has earned it the name "honeycomb coral."

Identification A colonial coral, usually massive. Individual coral animals ¹⁄₁₆″ long and wide, fitting together like cells in a honeycomb. Thin walls perforated by circular pores arranged in rows along each face. Partitions absent or represented by short rows of spines. Numerous horizontal platforms extend completely across each individual coral animal.

Age Late Ordovician to Middle Devonian.

Range Widespread in North America.

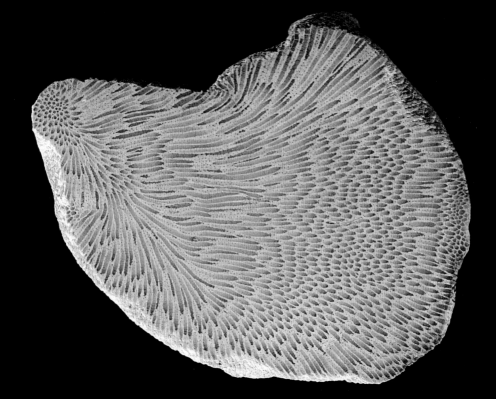

Heliophyllum

Locally abundant, *Heliophyllum* fossils show great variation in form caused by the age of the individual coral animals, their growth rates, and the nature of the sea floor sediments. As the living animal grew, the partitions in the skeleton to which the animal attached itself were added in groups of four. These partitions are usually still visible in the fossil.

Identification A solitary coral, 1¼″ long and wide, sometimes in small groups. Bowl-shaped, conical, or tubular. Outside heavily wrinkled. Deep bowl-shaped depression at top of coral. Many partitions with numerous small crossbars extend to center of coral; there are so many partitions it is difficult to see that they are arranged in groups of 4. In weathered specimens, partitions and crossbars create a latticelike appearance.

Age Early and Middle Devonian.

Range Widespread in eastern North America; rare in West.

Heterophrentis

In some places you can collect specimens of this coral without a hammer because the original skeleton, made of calcium carbonate, has been replaced by silica or quartz. The fossils are loose because rainwater, which is slightly acid, has dissolved away the surrounding limestone. Collectors can hasten nature's slow process by putting blocks of limestone into dilute hydrochloric acid, which will dissolve the limestone but not the fossils.

Identification   A solitary, usually slender, horn-shaped coral, 3½″ long, 2½″ wide. Top of coral with deep bowl-shaped depression; center raised slightly. Major partitions thicken towards edge of coral, become thinner towards center; minor partitions short.

Age   Early and Middle Devonian.

Range   Widespread in eastern North America.

Prismatophyllum

This beautiful coral, called the Petoskey Stone, is the official state stone of Michigan. It is often polished to show off its color and form and frequently made into jewelry. In worn specimens, there is usually a central, circular depression in each individual animal, or corallite. Petoskey Stones have also been called *Hexagonaria*. Changes in the width and shape of individual coral structures may indicate faster growth in summer and slower growth in winter. The age of the coral is estimated by counting the number of changes.

Identification : A massive, colonial coral, usually 6-sided; partitions thin with numerous small crossbars. Lower surface heavily wrinkled. Individual coral animal about ½″ long and wide.

Age : Early and Middle Devonian.

Range : Widespread in eastern North America; rare in West.

44

Halysites

When fossils of *Halysites* or "chain coral" are found, they are often preserved within reef limestones. This usually means that these corals are still in the position they held in life. Fossil reefs do not form layers because reefs grow continuously upward. But *Halysites* is also found in limestone that accumulates in front of a reef as a result of erosion by waves. Deposited here, these reef limestones display layers. *Halysites* often stands up in relief in weathered limestones.

Identification   A colonial coral. Individual coral animal 1⁄16″ long and wide, long and tubular, round or oval in cross section, joined together at sides to form chains that come together and diverge. Areas between chains open.

Age   Silurian.

Range   Widespread in North America.

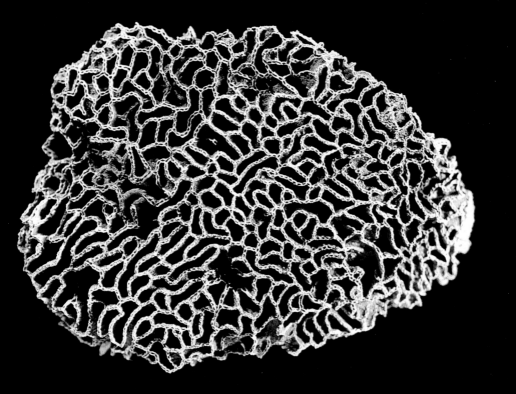

Meandrina

Because the surface of this boulderlike, colonial coral is covered with narrow, winding grooves, *Meandrina* is usually called the brain coral. It has been found as a fossil along the Gulf Coast and in the West Indies, but is better known as a living creature in these same places. In *Meandrina*, the individual animals live along the grooves and share a common digestive system; food captured by the tentacles of one animal nourishes other colony members.

Identification   A massive colonial coral up to 1′ in diameter, covered with many long, winding grooves lined with parallel partitions. Partitions of neighboring grooves meet to form zigzag, crestlike ridges. Individual coral animal ⅝″ long and wide.

Age   Miocene to Recent (perhaps also in Eocene).

Range   Gulf Coast of United States.

48

Aulopora

These fossil corals usually look like a network of interwoven chains. They also occur as crusts on the dorsal valves of brachiopods. Some paleontologists interpret this habit as a partnership in which the movements of the brachiopod brought food to *Aulopora* and the coral protected the brachiopod from enemies with its stinging cells. *Aulopora* lived in the warm, clear water of sheltered lagoons; it is usually found in fine-grained sediments that show no sign of wave action.

Identification   A colonial coral in the form of flat chains, networks, or crusts. Individual coral animals short, trumpet-shaped, ¼″ long and wide; each one growing outward from the side of another. Horizontal platforms characteristic of many other corals absent or rare.

Age   Late Ordovician to Pennsylvanian.

Range   Widespread in North America.

Syringopora

These fossils are not usually a major component of coral reefs, but may be locally abundant. Upright clusters of tubes attained heights and widths of two feet. *Syringopora* is often associated with a spongelike animal called *Stromatopora;* the two sometimes grew intimately together in reefs. Some scientists have interpreted this as a partnership in which the two animals shared food and were not harmful to one another.

Identification   A colonial coral forming loose bundles or clusters of nearly parallel cylinders. Individual coral animals ¼″ long and wide; long, cylindrical, thick-walled, and irregularly interconnected by small crossbars. Partitions short when present. Horizontal platforms funnel-shaped.

Age   Silurian to Early Permian.

Range   Widespread in North America.

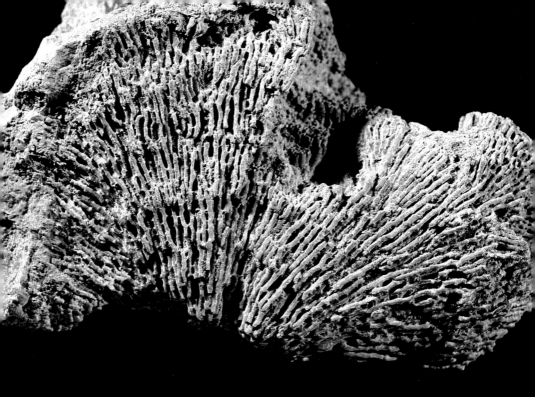

Fenestella

You cannot miss the lacy skeletons of this bryozoan or moss animal in fossil-bearing rocks. The fronds look like little screens made of a network of branches and connecting crossbars. The colonies grew upright and ranged from cup-shaped to fan-shaped. The individual animals moved their tentacles to create currents, and strained food material out of the water as it passed through the small openings.

Identification   Colony lacy, funnel-shaped, or fan-shaped, 1⅛″ high, 1¼″ wide; narrow, rigid, straight, or sinuous branches connected at fairly regular intervals by crossbars. Branches have 2 longitudinal rows of apertures on 1 side only. Individual animal ⅟₈₅″ long, ⅟₁₂₅″ wide.

Age   Silurian to Permian.

Range   Widespread in North America.

Stomatopora

This bryozoan has a long history, dating back to the Ordovician Period. It belongs to a group whose colonies have round apertures, and were one of the few groups of bryozoans to survive into the Mesozoic Era. During Jurassic times *Stomatopora* was widespread, encrusting any hard surface it could find. It had a wide tolerance for different materials and grew rapidly outward from its starting point. By late Cretaceous times *Stomatopora* had largely been replaced by other more aggressive bryozoans, but it is still with us today.

Identification Colony of tiny, branching, curving tubes, with round apertures in a line that are fairly evenly spaced. Individual animals ¹⁄₅₀″ long, ¹⁄₁₇₀″ wide.

Age Ordovician to Recent.

Range Widespread in North America.

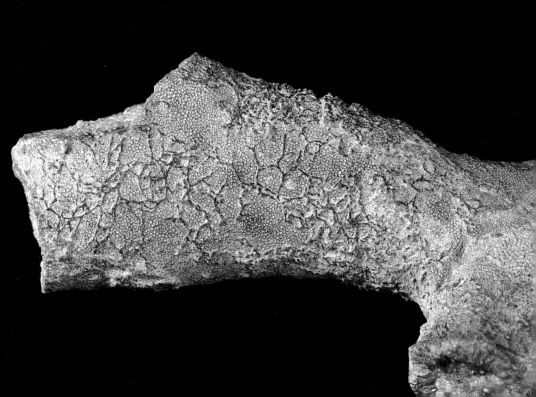

Ceriopora

Each of the apertures on the surface of a colony of *Ceriopora* once housed a small animal with tentacles for catching small particles of food. The members of a colony were connected by slender threads of tissue, but unlike most corals, each bryozoan had its own digestive system and did not share food with its neighbors. A colony began when a drifting larva settled on a rock or other hard surface; by budding off new animals, the larva became the parent of a new colony.

Identification   Colony ½″ high, ⅝″ wide. A rounded, crust-forming, or branching colonial bryozoan, with many apertures marking location of individual animals on surface but without small pores between apertures. Individual animal only ¹⁄₁₂₅″ long and wide.

Age   Triassic to Pliocene.

Range   Widespread in North America.

Rhombopora

A close look at a broken edge of the twiglike *Rhombopora* reveals outwardly radiating lines. These are tubes in which the members of the colony lived. They retracted into these tubes when resting or when under attack by a predator, and reached out with hairy tentacles to feed on tiny organisms filtered from the water. Fossil bryozoans can be confused with colonial corals, but are much smaller and do not have partitions.

Identification   Branches ⅝" long, ¹⁄₁₆" wide. Colony with solid, branching stems. Tube apertures oval and aligned in regular oblique rows. Surface slopes upward from tube apertures and ends in ridges of short spines. Intersecting ridges produce a rhomboid outline around each aperture. Individual animal ¹⁄₅₀" long and wide.

Age   Devonian to Permian.

Range   Widespread in North America.

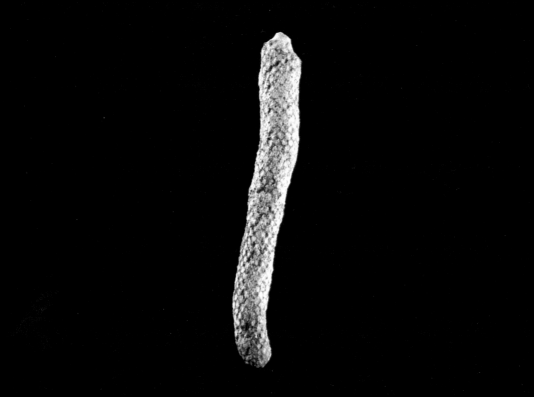

Archimedes

During part of the Mississippian Period, the middle of the continent was covered by a shallow, tropical sea with slowly migrating underwater sand banks. Here *Archimedes*, a bryozoan, thrived on the protected sides of shoals. As older colonies collapsed, new ones sprang up from the fragments. Studies show that colonies tended to fall over in the direction of the migrating sand banks; this allowed them to stay in the most sheltered places.

Identification Axis 4″ long, ⅛″ wide. Colony of latticelike branches and crossbars, with 2 longitudinal rows of animals on branches; none on crossbars. Colony supported by screwlike axis of layered, calcified tissue that held edge of lacy colony. Axis is often preserved alone. Individual animal ½₀″ long, ⅟₈₅″ wide.

Age Mississippian.

Range Widespread in North America.

Hydnoceras

Sponges have only a few kinds of cells, and these are not organized into tissues as in higher animals. They are filter feeders that live on the sea floor. *Hydnoceras* is related to the modern glass sponges that live in deep water, but is found in muddy sediments deposited in shallow water. The base of the sponge was firmly attached to the sea floor. Fossils of *Hydnoceras* are not the actual skeletons but casts of the skeleton created when the inside was filled with fine sediment.

Identification   8″ or more tall. Conical or vase-shaped and thin-walled, with pronounced, evenly spaced knobs at intersections of horizontal and vertical ridges. Outer surface covered by meshlike pattern of fine ridges made of tiny, mineralized skeletal elements called spicules.

Age   Late Devonian to Pennsylvanian.

Range   New York and Pennsylvania.

Hindia

The numerous small pores crowded on the surface of *Hindia* communicated with a dense network of narrow canals that led through the thick walls and into a central chamber deep inside the sponge. No stalk or other means of attachment to the bottom has been found in *Hindia*, and the fossils have no depression marking the top, such as is seen in most other sponges. This may mean that this spherical sponge didn't have a top or bottom and simply rolled about with the currents on the floor of the sea.

Identification 2¾″ long and wide. A round, smooth, thick-walled, stalkless sponge covered with many small pores and lacking the depression found at the top of *Astylospongia* and most other sponges.

Age Ordovician to Permian.

Range Eastern United States and Canada; Nevada.

66

Astylospongia

This sponge was melon-shaped, with pores leading into a central cavity. Water and food were carried into the cavity where the food was digested and the water passed out through an opening at the top. *Astylospongia* was the most common North American sponge. Small skeletal elements called spicules were fused together to make a strong mass that kept its shape even after the sponge died. The base of *Astylospongia* is rounded and there is no evidence this sponge was attached to the sea floor.

Identification   2″ long and wide. Spherical, sometimes bowl-shaped; hollow depression on upper surface; the large canal openings are parallel to surface; minor canals radiate from center of canal; outer surface grooved.

Age   Ordovician to Silurian.

Range   Iowa, Illinois, Indiana, Ohio, Ontario, and New York south to Kentucky and Tennessee.

Dendraster

One of the commonest creatures, easy to collect, on the beaches of the West Coast is the sand dollar, *Dendraster*. These inhabitants of sandy shores have also left a rich fossil record. In some sediments they are the main component of the rock. They have a life span of from 1 to 15 years, and increase dramatically in numbers whenever environmental conditions are just right. Mass deaths have been observed after spawning takes place. A small but constant percentage of sand dollar fossils shows damage due to attacks by crabs.

Identification 1¾″ long and wide. Skeleton almost circular and flattish. Five petal-shaped loops on top surface. Center of loops shifted toward front of animal. Covered with short, fine spines. Mouth in middle of lower surface.

Age Pliocene to Recent.

Range Puget Sound to Gulf of California.

Hemiaster

One of the heart urchins, *Hemiaster* specializes in burrowing. It digs a hole to sit in, then moves its fine, hairlike cilia about, to draw in fresh water and to gather small particles of food. Species of *Hemiaster* that lived near the equator during the Cretaceous Period had long petals with many tube feet. Those in more temperate climates had short petals with fewer tube feet. Because of these differences, fossils of *Hemiaster* can be used as environmental indicators, that is, they show what the ancient environment they lived in was like.

Identification 1½″ long, 1⅜″ wide. Heart-shaped, longer than wide, with flat base. Rear edge ends abruptly. Upper surface with 5 areas, 4 petal-shaped loops, 5th a broad, shallow depression. Mouth on base near front margin.

Age Early Cretaceous to Recent.

Range Widespread in North America.

Pentremites

To some, *Pentremites* looks like a flower bud, but it is really a blastoid, a stemmed animal with delicate arms. A study showed that *Pentremites* fossils from impure limestone were larger than those in pure limestone. This was thought to be due to a poorer food supply where the impure limestone was being formed—the animals grew larger to raise water intake and make up for the smaller amount of food. But then at other sites of the same age, *Pentremites* specimens were found to be the same size in both kinds of limestone. This contradiction shows how theories must change as new discoveries are made.

Identification | 1¼″ high, 1″ wide. Conical, and wide at the base; 5-sided in cross section. Five U-shaped depressions on sides. Mouth at top, surrounded by 5 round holes.

Age | Mississippian to Permian.

Range | Widespread in North America.

Glyptocrinus

One of the most common and typical fossil crinoids—
stemmed animals with delicate arms—*Glyptocrinus* had
a cup-shaped body with branched arms and was mounted
on a stem attached to the sea floor by a "root system."
The stem was somewhat flexible, allowing the crinoid to
bend with the current. The rigid cup was formed of five-
and six-sided plates arranged in rings, and contained
most of the soft parts. The mouth was in the center of
the upper surface. The arms had grooves lined with cilia
facing toward the mouth; these grooves were also lined
with tube feet for respiration and trapping tiny one-
celled plants and animals. The food was swept down the
grooves to the mouth by the motion of the cilia.

Identification 2⅜″ high, 3⅛″ wide. A high conical body with circle of
5-sided base plates. Twenty free arms.

Age Middle Ordovician to Silurian.

Range Widespread in North America.

Crinoid Stems

The stem of a crinoid consists of a stack of rounded or five-sided disks. A stalk may be built of disks of several shapes and sizes. Each disk is marked above and below with many interlocking ridges and grooves. In the center of each disk is a hole for an extension of the soft parts of the animal. Crinoid fossils in limestones are composed almost entirely of these disks, either separate or joined together in short lengths. They look like checkers after a game, some loose and scattered, others in neat stacks.

Identification	¼″ long, ⅛″ wide. Small disks, usually round but may be 5-sided, single or stacked. Hole in center may be round or 5-looped. Upper and lower surface of disk with grooves and ridges arranged radially.
Age	Early Ordovician to Recent.
Range	Widespread in North America.

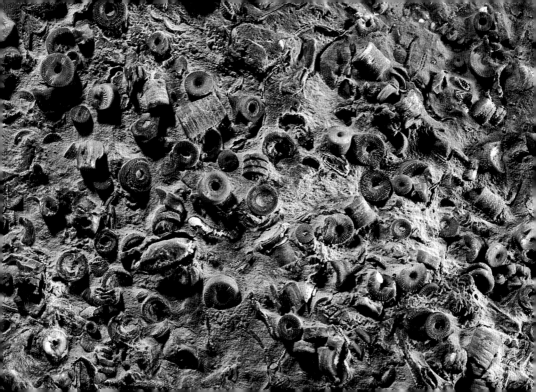

Tentaculites

Although the details of its structure are well known, very little is known about the way *Tentaculites* lived. Scientists are not sure just what kind of an animal it was, but this hasn't stopped them from speculating. It has been suggested that *Tentaculites* was a filter feeder, and that its ringed shell helped it anchor in the sediment. These animals lived in shallow, tropical seas. When found, the fossils are usually abundant and often lie nearly parallel to one another in the sediment.

Identification   ¾″ long, ⅛″ wide. A small, straight, gently tapering cone with rings covering the outside of its shell. Rings generally increase in size and number towards the aperture. Chamber inside long and conical.

Age   Early Silurian to Late Devonian (perhaps also in Early Ordovician).

Range   Widespread in North America.

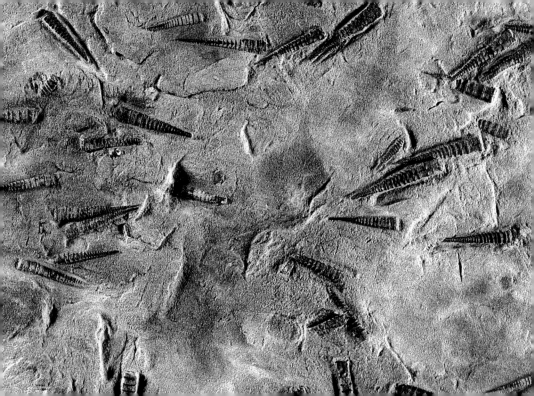

Belemnitella

It is always surprising after digging in sandy silt all day to turn up what looks like a bunch of cigars. These curious fossils are the internal shells or guards that served as ballast for tentacled, flesh-eating marine animals that are similar to present-day cuttlefish and squid. Another part of the skeleton, not found as often, had partitions pierced by a long tube, and fit into the cavity of the larger guard. In the past Europeans called the guards "Devil's thunderbolts."

Identification   4″ long, ½″ wide. A long, narrow cone, usually light to dark brown and sometimes glassy, with circular cross section. Tip blunt; wide end with cavity. Long groove down side toward apex. Growth layers like tree rings visible inside cavity when sectioned.

Age   Cretaceous.

Range   Widespread in North America.

Baculites

This beautiful fossil is often found with its iridescent shell still intact and etched by complex sutures. *Baculites* is unusual among cephalopods—relatives of squids and octopuses—in having the shell straight and not distinctly coiled. Only a tiny coil remains at the tip, and the sutures are more intricate than in most other cephalopods. Not much is known about the life of *Baculites*, but they were the prey of plesiosaurs, large marine lizards that flourished in Cretaceous seas.

Identification 3¾" long, 1¼" wide. Shell long, straight, and tapering. Tip may have short spiral curve. Shell smooth or with weak ribs. Suture lines symmetrical with complex folding; suture lines usually 6" long, but sometimes 6'.

Age Late Cretaceous.

Range Widespread in North America.

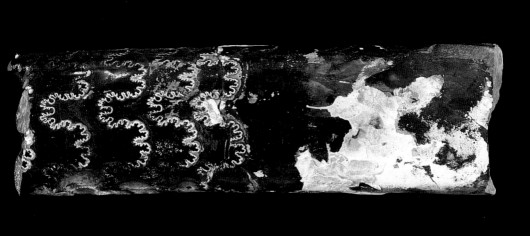

Endoceras

This early relative of squids was one of the first shelled predators, feeding on snails and other invertebrates. Some of its close relatives had chambered shells 30 feet long, making them the largest of all Paleozoic fossils. In these ancient cephalopods the most delicate part of the shell was often the siphuncle, the tube connecting all of the chambers. But in *Endoceras* this is the part most often preserved, because inside the tip of the shell there are deposits, stacked like paper cups in a dispenser, that strengthen the shell and are easily seen when it is split open.

Identification 11¾″ long, ¾″ wide. A large, heavy, and straight cone-shaped shell that is nearly cylindrical. Sutures between chambers simple and straight.

Age Middle and Late Ordovician.

Range Widespread in North America.

Turritella

In the fine-grained rock where you find *Turritella*, the
thin layers of sediment are often uneven and disturbed.
They are broken up into swirls and loops because many
animals living on the sea floor have the ability to disturb
the bedding. Modern *Turritella* feeds in sediment by
stirring up the mud to find minute animals, and burrows
into the bottom so deeply that sometimes only the tip of
its narrow shell can be seen. The snail moves about by
slowly arching its fleshy foot like an inchworm, while its
long shell drags behind along the sea floor. All these
activities further disturb the layers of sediment.

Identification 2″ high, ½″ wide. A long, slender shell coiled with many
turns and ornamented with spiral ribbing; aperture
somewhat angular; inside of shell smooth.

Age Triassic to Recent.

Range Widespread in North America.

Loxonema

This graceful snail is usually found with brachiopods, an indication that like them, *Loxonema* lived in shallow tropical seas, where it scoured the muddy sea floor for vegetation. When *Loxonema* is fossilized, its three-dimensional shape is often destroyed by the weight of the overlying sediments, and the shell is flattened like a pancake. When you find a *Loxonema*, you can see that, as in most snails, its shell is a coiled tube.

Identification   Up to 3½" high. A long, turreted shell with a high, pointed spire consisting of many rounded turns, and ornamented with wavy growth lines. Aperture long, enlarged in the front, and containing a shallow canal. Outer lip thin and curved, with deep, U-shaped depression.

Age   Ordovician to Mississippian.

Range   Widespread in North America.

Conus

A carnivorous snail, *Conus* still lives on sandy sea floors, where it shoots poison darts at its prey. *Conus* is one of the most popular shells among shell collectors because of its shape and the variety of its colors and patterns. Some specimens of fossil *Conus* have been found with their color patterns preserved, and others have color patterns that can only be seen under ultraviolet light. The fossils are usually white and chalky, but may have a shiny luster.

Identification   1½–5″ high. Conical and generally smooth, with coil covering greater part of shell. Spire short, and flat or conical, with many turns. Aperture long, narrow, and straight, with nearly parallel borders. Shell thick on outside, but inner parts often very thin.

Age   Cretaceous to Recent.

Range   Widespread in North America.

Busycon

Shells of *Busycon* are easily found on many beaches today. There are many living species and they are usually called whelks. *Busycon* is a common fossil, but it is usually difficult to find one that is not broken, because after an animal died, unless it was buried rapidly, it was tossed around in the currents on the sea floor. *Busycon* is a predator; it feeds on other snails and bivalves. It holds its prey with its fleshy foot and bangs it sharply against its own sturdy outer lip until the shell of its victim cracks.

Identification   5" high, 2¼" wide. A large, heavy, pear-shaped shell, smooth or with strong spiral lines. Ribs often present, and sometimes spines on shoulders at each turn of the coil. Aperture pear-shaped.

Age   Late Cretaceous to Recent.

Range   Widespread in North America.

Cancellaria

Fossils of *Cancellaria* are usually found in muddy or sandy sediments that have been undisturbed by wave action and currents. It lives today at depths of as much as 50 feet, or in shallow water in beds of turtle-grass. The tiny teeth of modern *Cancellaria* are shaped like slender blades of grass and the animal probably uses them to feed on soft, sand-dwelling animals. *Cancellaria* has a strong shell and fossils are often found unbroken.

Identification   ½" high, ⅝" wide. Shell an inflated oval with 6 or 7 coils. Spire usually less than half total length of shell. Aperture crescent-shaped, with short, deep notch. Ribs cross one another on surface nearly at right angles, producing a cross-hatched effect.

Age   Miocene to Recent (perhaps also Cretaceous).

Range   Atlantic, Pacific, and Gulf coastal plains.

Ecphora

In the places along the Atlantic Coast where *Ecphora* is found, it is the most popular fossil after sharks' teeth. It is usually preserved in loose sediment rather than rocks, and is frequently found unbroken. The shell of *Ecphora* has two layers. The brown outer layer is composed of the mineral calcite and the thin, pale inner layer is made of aragonite. Aragonite is a less stable mineral and this is why it is not unusual to find the inner layer of *Ecphora* dissolved away.

Identification 2⅛" high, 1⅞" wide. A loosely coiled shell with low spire. Turns of coil have flat shoulders and usually 4 distinctive ribs. Aperture oval, narrowing into long canal that ends in a notch. Outer lip wavy. Opening below axis of coil broad and deep.

Age Cretaceous to Miocene.

Range Atlantic and Gulf coastal plains.

Worthenia

This turban-shaped snail lived in shallow water and can be found as a fossil in many kinds of sedimentary rock. *Worthenia* was a grazer, and fed on algae growing on the sea floor. Many species and relatives of *Worthenia* look almost exactly like it, and only a detailed study of the structure of the shells will distinguish them. Several modern relatives of *Worthenia* were discovered during the 19th century and these seashells are highly prized by collectors.

Identification 1⅛″ high, 1″ wide. A top-shaped or turban-shaped snail. Aperture squarish, with slit. Coil angular with flattened surfaces; each turn of coil has strongly ridged shoulder with small bumps. As the shell grew, the slit filled with shell material and left a band on the coil.

Age Mississippian to Middle Triassic.

Range Widespread in North America.

Bellerophon

The sediments in which *Bellerophon* is found were deposited in warm waters where waves and currents were not strong, and where it probably made its living by grazing on the sea floor. Nothing is known about its soft anatomy, but many of its features are considered primitive clues to the early evolution of the snails.

Identification Up to 3″ in diameter. Globular, smooth, and often with growth lines. Aperture oval or nearly circular, and tending to flare out along front margin. Opening between coils small or closed, and shell symmetrically coiled in 1 plane. The number of coils is small, and the latest coil covers the earlier ones. The edge of the aperture contains a deep slit; as the snail grew the slit became a band dividing the shell into 2 symmetrical parts.

Age Silurian to Early Triassic.

Range Widespread in North America.

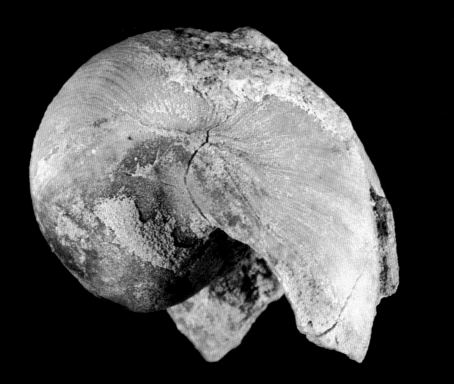

Platyceras

One of the most common snails in the Paleozoic Era, *Platyceras* had a very interesting life history. It attached itself to crinoids and fed on their waste material. The relationship was so close that each kind of snail was found on a particular species of crinoid. The growth lines on the snail's shell match the details of the crinoid, and often the snails are so well hidden between the arm bases of the crinoid that you have to remove the arms to find them. When a crinoid died, the snail was forced to live on the sea floor, and so its fossils are often found unattached.

Identification	1″ high and wide. Shell variable in shape, ranging from a tight coil to an open one. Shell thin, with fine growth lines. Shape of aperture variable.
Age	Silurian to Middle Permian.
Range	Widespread in North America.

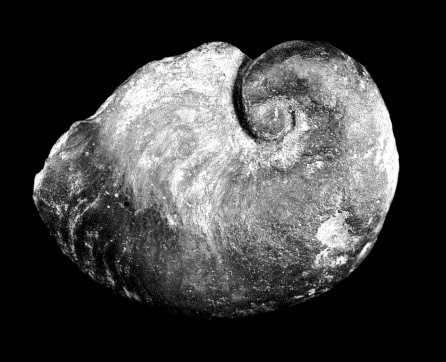

Exogyra

Huge shell banks formed of *Exogyra* are not uncommon in Cretaceous sediments along the Gulf Coast. They flourished in shallow, warm, marine environments. One species has been found from New Jersey to Mexico, a distance of 2,500 miles. *Exogyra* attached itself to a hard object such as a shell fragment on the sea floor, and some species grew so large that they weighed much more than the object they were attached to and became virtually free-living.

Identification   3½″ long, 4″ high. Similar to *Ostrea*, with shell attached to sea floor by large, massive left valve. Beak of left valve curved back into coil. Right valve flat, sometimes like cap or cover. Growth lines heavy, sometimes with ribs.

Age   Cretaceous.

Range   Atlantic Coast; Gulf coastal plain to Utah.

Maclurites

These fossil snails were abundant in the Ordovician Period, but are seldom well preserved. You can often recognize them easily in cut limestone because their cross sections look like large, loosely coiled springs. *Maclurites* is usually found associated with reefs that were built of corals, algae, and sponges. They lived on the reef by grazing algae, and when they died the algae often encrusted their shells. Cephalopods were among their enemies. Shells of *Maclurites* are often found piled together in ancient channels on the reefs, brought together by currents.

Identification Commonly 4–5″ in diameter; occasionally up to 8″. A large, disk-shaped shell with flat base; last turn of coil large. Space at axis of coiling wide and deep.

Age Ordovician.

Range Widespread in North America.

Gastrioceras

Beginning collectors sometimes get coiled cephalopods mixed up with snails. Cephalopods are chambered animals, and snails have an uninterrupted, coiled shell. One of the chambered cephalopods, *Gastrioceras* is recognized by the shape of the sutures at the junction between the inside of the shell and the walls of the chambers; the sutures are generally sharp and angular and there are usually eight lobes on each coil. *Gastrioceras* lived for about ten million years, and this makes it a valuable fossil to use for dating rock formations.

Identification   ⅝" long, ⅜" wide; occasionally 1¼" long, ¾" wide. A coiled shell with large depression at axis of coiling. Shell marked with strong ribs on inner margins. Suture line usually divided into 8 angular lobes.

Age   Pennsylvanian.

Range   Widespread in North America.

Placenticeras

The most famous fossil of *Placenticeras* is a 12-inch specimen that was bitten 16 times by a predatory marine lizard called a mosasaur. Tooth marks on the shell show that the lizard attacked this cephalopod from above and appears to have been trying to swallow it. Eventually the chamber was broken and the empty shell sank to the sea floor. We don't know if *Placenticeras* was a regular prey of the sea-going mosasaurs. The feeding habits of both *Placenticeras* and its possible predators are poorly known.

Identification 9½" long, 2⅜" wide. A disk-shaped shell with strong, overlapping turns, very complex sutures, and a deep pit at axis of coiling. Weak sculpture of faint ribs present in young stages, absent in older specimens.

Age Late Cretaceous.

Range Widespread in North America.

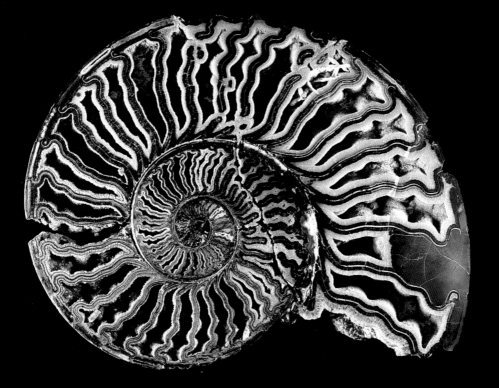

Eutrephoceras

This cephalopod survived until the Miocene Period, and was one of the most advanced members of the group. The shell is tightly coiled and has simple sutures. When you find fossil *Eutrephoceras* shells, the chambers are partially or completely filled with sediment or crystals of calcite. In life the chambers were filled with gas and the animal lived in the largest and outermost chamber. The modern cephalopod *Nautilus* swims by jet propulsion and *Eutrephoceras* probably did also.

Identification 2⅛" long, 1¾" wide. Shell tightly coiled and almost spherical, with last coil completely covering earlier ones. Aperture broad and shallow. Surface smooth with fine growth lines.

Age Late Jurassic through Miocene.

Range Widespread in coastal areas and western interior of North America.

Temnocheilus

The buoyancy of chambered cephalopods is unlike that of fishes. Fishes have a swim bladder containing gas at a pressure equal to that of the water. Modern *Nautilus* maintains its position in the water by controlling the amount of liquid in the chambers. Removal of the liquid through the siphuncle makes the shell more buoyant, and the shell rises. *Temnocheilus*, one of the earliest and most primitive of the coiled cephalopods, may have controlled its buoyancy this way too.

Identification 1¼″ long, ⅜″ wide. A flat, disk-shaped coil with turns just touching and with hole in center. Siphuncle almost in center of chambers. Shoulders of turns ornamented with a single row of large, elongate bumps.

Age Mississippian through Permian.

Range Kentucky, Illinois, Missouri, Kansas, Texas, and Colorado.

Chesapecten

Until recently, the snail *Ecphora* was thought to be the first North American fossil to be described, but this honor rightfully belongs to *Chesapecten*, which was illustrated and described in 1687. *Chesapecten* lived on the sea floor on its flattened right valve at depths ranging from a few feet down to 131 feet. Like modern scallops, it was able to escape enemies by swimming for a short time, vigorously flapping its valves. Its name comes from Chesapeake Bay, where its fossils are abundant.

Identification 5½″ long, 5⅛″ high. Shell large, thick, and scallop-shaped. Both valves convex, left valve more so. Shells slightly longer than high. Usually bears 10–16 large ribs with many finer ribs between and on the surface of the major ribs.

Age Miocene through Pliocene.

Range Atlantic coastal plain.

Mercenaria

This bivalve is a common fossil that lived in shallow water just below the tide line and to depths of 120 feet. The modern species was used by Native Americans for wampum and beads. It burrows actively in soft sandy sediment; in shallow water it is found near the surface but at low tide it burrows more deeply. This is a common commercial clam, known by a variety of names such as Cherrystone and Little Neck. In some deposits, fossils of this clam are as common as its present-day shells on a beach.

Identification   Up to 5″ long, 3⅛″ high. A thick shell with convex, oval valves. Shell smooth or ornamented concentrically and sometimes with radial ribs. Beaks small and pointed forward. Inside smooth, with 3 teeth just under beak, and fine line with shallow indentation near edge of valve, marking attachment of soft tissue.

Age   Oligocene to Recent.

Range   Atlantic and Gulf coastal plains.

Glycimeris

When you find fossil shells of *Glycimeris*, they are usually in sand or gravel sediments deposited by rapidly moving currents. We know much about *Glycimeris* because this bivalve is still alive today. It lacks siphon tubes, used by most burrowing clams to reach the surface for breathing and for taking in particles of food. Instead, *Glycimeris* lives on the sea floor only partially covered by sand. In coarser sediments, *Glycimeris* burrows more deeply and filters food from water that flows through the gravel.

Identification   1⅝″ long, 1½″ high. An almost circular shell with beaks located in center; fine radiating ribs and concentric growth lines on outside; numerous teeth along slightly curved hinge line on inside.

Age   Early Cretaceous to Recent.

Range   Widespread in North America.

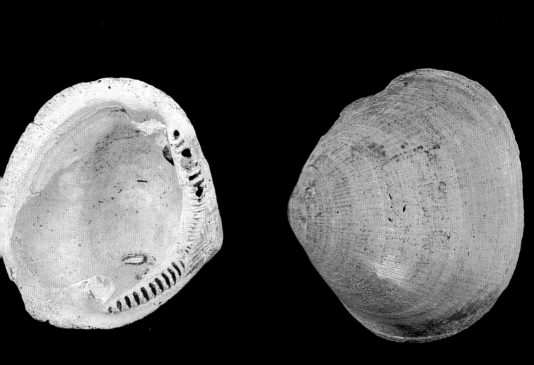

Nucula

The fossil record of *Nucula* is abundant. This bivalve is commonly found fossilized with many other invertebrates. When it is found with animals such as oysters that live on hard surfaces, we know that *Nucula* lived in pockets of sediment in adjacent lower places on the sea floor. The modern *Nucula* is called the Nut Shell and is usually found in colder water. *Nucula* lives just below the surface and feeds with special structures that collect food particles by "licking" the muddy sediment.

Identification   1⅛″ long, ¾″ high. Many species just ¼″. A triangular to oval shell, polished on inside and often pearly. Valves equal in size; lower edges with fine interlocking grooves and ridges. Beaks narrow and turned backward, with comblike teeth on each side.

Age   Late Cretaceous to Recent.

Range   Widespread in North America.

Rangia

Modern species of *Rangia* live in estuaries, where mixing of seawater with rain and fresh water from the land lowers the salt content of the water. These modern *Rangia* are used as an indicator of estuarine conditions, where the salinity is lower than it is in the sea. In some fossil deposits, however, *Rangia* clearly lived in a normal, shallow, marine environment. These fossils are used to indicate closeness to land. Ancient *Rangia* must have had a greater tolerance for salt water, and any larvae washed out into a saltier environment were able to survive.

Identification	2⅛" long, 2⅜" high. A thick, almost triangular shell with equal valves and prominent beaks that are tilted forward; shell with or without growth lines.
Age	Miocene to Recent (possibly also in Paleocene).
Range	Chesapeake Bay south to Texas.

Ostrea

Fossil *Ostrea* is usually preserved in its living position in belts parallel to the shoreline. These belts can be used to determine the location of ancient shorelines and bays. Modern *Ostrea* lives just below the tidal zone. Young oysters are swimming larvae that eventually settle down on a clean hard rock or shell. A gland then secretes a cement that fastens the left valve to the rock. As the young oysters grow, they mold themselves to the surface.

Identification 4¾" long, 5⅛" high. An irregular, generally round to elongate shell with narrow hinge. Left valve attached to hard surface, usually with radiating ribs, and larger than flat or concave and often smooth right valve.

Age Cretaceous to Recent.

Range Widespread in North America.

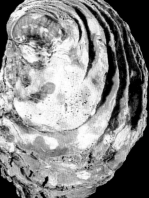

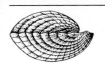

Lingula

Almost unchanged for 400 million years, *Lingula* is an example of a "living fossil." Brachiopods that live on the sea floor are either attached by a stalk, cemented to hard objects, fastened by spines, or unattached. *Lingula* possesses a flexible stalk that is attached to the bottom of a vertical burrow. Modern *Lingula* usually lives in fine sediment in the shallow, intertidal zone, and thrives in both brackish water and normal seawater. Fossil *Lingula* lived in a greater variety of environments, including deep water.

Identification 1″ long, ½″ wide. Valves thin, equal in size, smooth or with fine growth lines, and often black and shiny; generally shaped like a spade or tongue.

Age Silurian to Recent (possibly also in the Ordovician).

Range Widespread in North America.

Pentamerus

Fossil *Pentamerus* is usually found preserved as the animals lived, in large clusters or beds. In some large clusters of *Pentamerus*, the individuals were packed together so tightly that they touched one another, and as a result the shells were deformed by their neighbors as they grew. *Pentamerus* and its relatives were dominant brachiopods in water of moderate depths and their clusters were probably like the oyster reefs of today.

Identification 4″ long, 3¾″ wide. Valves large, long or tongue-shaped, moderately convex, and smooth outside; held together with teeth and sockets. Inside of lower valve smooth but with raised platform near hinge for attachment of muscle.

Age Silurian.

Range Anticosti Island, Quebec, New York, Ontario, Ohio, Indiana, Kentucky, Wisconsin, Illinois, and Iowa.

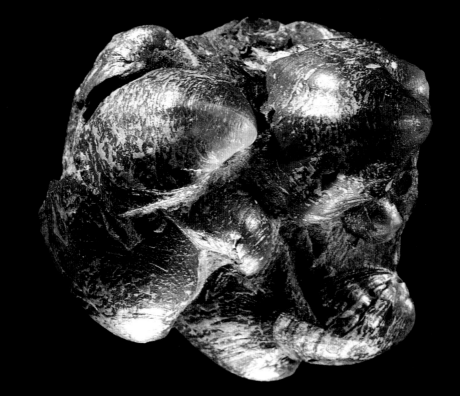

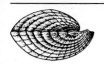

Orbiculoidea

Easily identified by its shape, *Orbiculoidea* is often associated with graptolites in the fossil record. The graptolites floated and *Orbiculoidea* attached itself to floating plants with a stalk. After death, *Orbiculoidea* and the graptolites drifted to the bottom, where they were preserved in black shales. Brachiopods like this one that hold their shells together with muscles are among the earliest brachiopods. They increased in numbers in the Ordovician but then declined.

Identification   ¼" long and wide. Valves small and nearly circular; upper valve cone-shaped, with point near center. Lower valve less conical, with slot for stalk and small triangular pit near edge; growth lines either weak or strong.

Age   Ordovician through Permian.

Range   Widespread in North America.

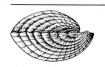

Athyris

Fossil valves of *Athyris* often stand out clearly in fine-grained sediments because of their whitish appearance. Individuals of *Athyris* lived alone, attached to the sea floor by a flexible stalk and resting obliquely on the upper valve. *Athyris* was one of the earliest brachiopods capable of removing some of the shell material away from the opening through which the stalk emerged, allowing the stalk to increase in size as the animal grew. In some other brachiopods that could not remove this shell material, the stalk eventually became useless, and the animal lived on the sea floor unattached.

Identification 1⅛" long, 1¼" wide. Shell nearly circular, oval, or 5-sided. Both valves convex, lower valve with grooves, upper valves with folds; growth lines weak. Valves held together by teeth and sockets.

Age Early Devonian through Mississippian.

Range Widespread in North America.

Productella

A common brachiopod in many environments, *Productella* was one of the earliest forms with spines. The spines usually broke off before or during fossilization, leaving only bases that may be difficult to see. *Productella* used the spines for attachment and for stabilizing itself on the sea floor. Some of the spines were filled with soft tissues and may have acted as sense organs, perhaps to detect predators.

Identification 7/8″ long, 1¼″ wide. Valves nearly circular, with fine ribs. Lower valve very convex, with spines scattered over surface; upper valve slightly concave. Hinge line shorter than width of shell. Valves held together by small teeth and sockets.

Age Middle and Late Devonian.

Range Western Canada and western United States; Ontario, New York, and Appalachian Mountains.

Terebratulina

The fossil record of *Terebratulina* suggests that it may have had a narrower habitat in the past than it does today. Although the fossil lived in relatively shallow water, today this brachiopod is found from just below the tidal zone to depths of 12,500 feet, where it clings to rocks and broken shells with its tufted stalk. However, deep-sea fossil deposits are not often found, but *Terebratulina* may have lived in the ocean depths in ancient times, too. *Terebratulina* is found today along the North Atlantic Coast from Labrador to New Jersey. Its common name is the North Atlantic Lamp Shell.

Identification ½" long, ⅜" wide. Valves oval or 5-sided. Both valves convex; surface with very fine radiating ridges. Valves held together by teeth and sockets.

Age Late Jurassic to Recent.

Range Widespread in North America.

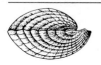

Desquamatia

Especially in weathered shale, you can find this
brachiopod in large numbers. They can be removed from
the rock with little effort. This is a widespread group
that lived in many habitats, from sandy sea bottoms to
hollows in reefs. In the past, *Desquamatia* and its
relatives were all called *Atrypa*. After collecting many
specimens of *Atrypa* from a number of localities, one
could not help noticing how variable the shell was in
shape, number of ribs and growth lines, and thickness.
The name *Desquamatia* was given to those fossils that
have fine ribs and weak growth lines.

Identification 1⅜" long and wide. Valves convex, upper valve more
convex, with beak slightly curved; growth lines weak.
Valves held together by teeth and sockets.

Age Devonian.

Range Widespread in North America.

Gypidula

This brachiopod is usually preserved in small clusters in mud that was deposited in quiet places, perhaps in sheltered lagoons. Since its fleshy stalk did not function, it had no means of fixing itself securely to the sea floor. When specimens are entombed in fine-grained limestone, they are easily collected; this type of limestone usually weathers rapidly and releases the fossils quickly.

Identification 1″ long and wide. Valves convex, nearly circular or oval. Beak of lower valve large and curved over upper valve. Ribs in middle of shell become smoother at sides. Lower valve with well-developed fold; upper valve with strong groove. Valves held together by teeth and sockets.

Age Middle and Late Devonian.

Range Widespread in North America.

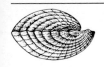

Schizophoria

Common in the Devonian, *Schizophoria* usually lived in groups in fine sediments. Although modern brachiopods are sometimes attached to soft mud with their stalks, we do not know if fossil species could fix themselves to a soft bottom. When the fossils are preserved where they lived, they are usually in groups. The first ones anchored themselves to a shell and after death provided a place of attachment for later arrivals. This suggests that they could not adhere to the soft sea floor.

Identification ¾" long, 1" wide. Both valves convex, nearly circular or angular in outline, elliptical in profile, and with fine ribs. Upper valve more convex than lower and with low fold; lower valve with groove. Valves held together with simple, strong teeth and sockets.

Age Silurian to Permian.

Range Widespread in North America.

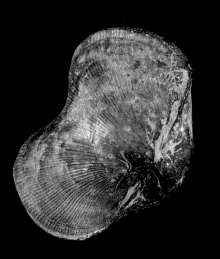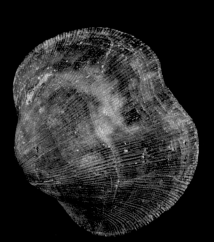

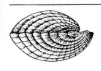

Hebertella

Modern brachiopods cannot tolerate too much sediment. To sweep out silt they must reverse the flow of water that brings them food particles. The convex shape of *Hebertella* enabled it to remain attached to the sea floor but kept the opening between the valves high enough to prevent sediment from clogging the shell. Its valves are abundant and usually found in bands or zones; where the fossil lived may have depended on the speed of currents, amount of sediment, and perhaps temperature.

Identification 1¼" long, 1¾" wide. Oval in profile with radiating ribs. Lower valve faintly convex or concave and with groove; upper valve strongly convex and with wide fold. Hinge line wide. Valves held together by teeth and sockets.

Age Middle and Late Ordovician.

Range Widespread in eastern North America.

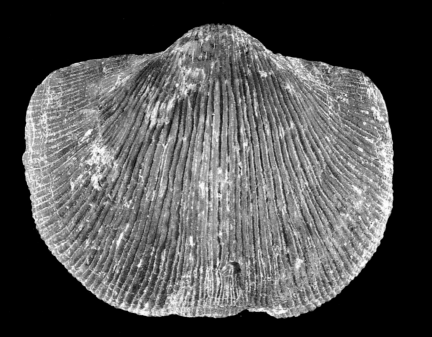

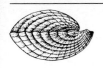

Rafinesquina

This brachiopod was part of a shallow-water community that also included crinoids, snails, gastropods, and trilobites, as well as other brachiopods. Although many of the brachiopods were attached to the sea floor, *Rafinesquina* rested on its lower valve and was not attached by its stalk. Swift currents could pick it up and sweep it away. We do not know how *Rafinesquina* survived under these conditions.

Identification ⅞″ long, 1⅛″ wide. Valves thin and flat; lower valve convex; upper valve concave and flatter. Hinge line nearly straight, rest of shell circular. Surface marked with both coarse and fine ribs; usually with very thick ribs down center. Valves held together by teeth and sockets.

Age Middle to Late Ordovician.

Range Widespread in North America.

Eoorthis

This fossil and its relatives were the forerunners of all other brachiopods with teeth and sockets. *Eoorthis* was one of the most abundant brachiopods during the Cambrian Period, and in some places there are layers many inches thick composed entirely of their shells. *Eoorthis* may have lived in huge assemblages like present-day oyster beds, or perhaps they were attached to algae in vast underwater meadows and accumulated in large numbers as they died.

Identification   ½" long, ¾" wide. Outline rectangular or circular, with long, straight hinge line. Both valves convex, with broad radial ribs marked with finer ribs. Valves held together by strong teeth and sockets.

Age   Late Cambrian.

Range   Montana, Wyoming, Minnesota, Wisconsin, Missouri, Oklahoma, and Texas.

Derbyia

Although *Derbyia* was attached to the sea floor early in its life, it was unattached when it became an adult. There are no unattached brachiopods surviving today, but during the Paleozoic Era they were common. We don't know how *Derbyia* lived, but perhaps when sediment accumulated in the opening between the valves, some vigorous clapping of the valves may have cleared it away. Such clapping might even have been a means of moving about, as it is for scallops today.

Identification 1″ long, 1¼″ wide. Both valves convex and marked with fine ribs. Lower valve variable in shape, with long, narrow, bladelike partition. Valves held together by teeth and sockets.

Age Mississippian to Permian.

Range Nevada, Nebraska, Kansas, Iowa, Missouri, Oklahoma, Texas, Ohio, Indiana, Kentucky, and southern Appalachian Mountains.

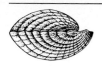

Platystrophia

This distinctive brachiopod was attached to sand or mud by its flexible stalk. Where the interior of shell is exposed, often the supports for the lophophore—the main food-gathering and respiratory organ—are preserved. The supports extend down from the top of the upper valve. The lophophore consisted of a pair of grooved lobes or arms with tentacles fringed with fine hairs. Most of the interior of the brachiopod was filled up by it.

Identification   ¾″ long, 1¼″ wide. Valves strongly convex, almost rectangular in outline, widest at hinge line or at middle of valves, and marked with many sharp ribs. Upper valve with deep fold; lower valve with groove. Valves held together with simple teeth and sockets.

Age   Middle Ordovician to Late Silurian.

Range   Widespread in North America.

Mucrospirifer

Occasionally sandstone is found with bedding layers that are covered with the valves of *Mucrospirifer*. They are usually not oriented and their external surfaces face upward. *Mucrospirifer* was a solitary brachiopod attached by a stalk, and with the top of the shell oriented downward, so these fossils are not preserved in their living position. They have been carried to a site of deposition.

Identification   ½″ long, 1⅝″ wide. Valves very wide and usually sharply pointed at hinge line. Outline often 5-sided; top of shell turned inward. Upper valve with prominent fold; lower valve with groove and small opening for stalk. Valves held together with teeth and sockets.

Age   Middle Devonian.

Range   New York and Appalachian Mountains.

Leptaena

One of the commonest brachiopods, *Leptaena* is also among the most easily recognized. Most species lay free on the sea floor. There are two explanations of how *Leptaena* lived: *Leptaena* may have stabilized itself by inserting the downturned edge of the shell into the mud as a brace, but if this is true, it could not have eaten in this position. A more plausible explanation is that it rested on its lower valve, with the bent portion turned upward, raising its opening above the sediment so it could eat and breathe.

Identification   ¾″ long, ⅞″ wide. Valves nearly rectangular to semicircular in outline, with fine ribs and concentric wrinkles. Hinge line straight, often with extensions on either side. Lower valve slightly convex, upper valve flat. Front edges of both valves L-shaped, bending in direction of upper valve. Valves held together by teeth and sockets.

Age   Middle Ordovician to Devonian.

Range   Widespread in North America.

Homotelus

As *Homotelus* burrowed through the sediment, it may have obtained food by drawing in mud and extracting the organic matter. At one locality a fine-grained limestone is covered with the fossilized remains of *Homotelus*. The skeletons are oriented in every way and many are upside down. Currents carried the bodies of these trilobites to the site of deposition after some calamity killed them. The currents must have been gentle because they show no signs of abrasion.

Identification	5″ long, 2¾″ wide. Skeleton oval, with 8 body segments. Head and tail about the same size and shape, both triangular in outline. Head smooth, with central area barely visible. Eyes large and semicircular.
Age	Late Ordovician.
Range	Ohio.

Phacops

One of the best-known trilobites, *Phacops* is often beautifully preserved. Specimens from some localities are quickly exposed because the limestone is easily removed. The eyes of *Phacops* are prominent and unlike anything else in the animal kingdom. Each element of the compound eyes was corrected for astigmatism and adapted for night vision, allowing the animal to see 360 degrees, and giving it three-dimensional vision. *Phacops* had stout walking legs and some of the appendages under the head may have been used for crushing food.

Identification   1⅝" long, ¾" wide. Skeleton oval, with 11 equal segments. Central region of head raised, widest at front, and with many bumps. Eyes large and crescent-shaped. Tail semicircular, with rounded edges.

Age   Devonian.

Range   Widespread in North America.

Olenoides

Well preserved in shale in British Columbia, *Olenoides* is one of the few trilobites whose limbs have survived intact. The antennae and tail appendages are composed of many jointed rings and the tail appendages also bear minute hairs; they may have had some sensory function. There were three pairs of legs under the head, seven under the body, and four to six under the tail. Each leg had one part for walking and another with feathery structures used for respiration and possibly in swimming.

Identification 1⅝″ long, 1⅜″ wide. Skeleton oval, with 7–8 equal body segments ending in short spines. Spines on side of head short. Central part of head with 3 pairs of furrows, and with small adjacent eyes. Tail same size as head, with slender marginal spines.

Age Middle Cambrian (possibly also in Late Cambrian).

Range Widespread in North America.

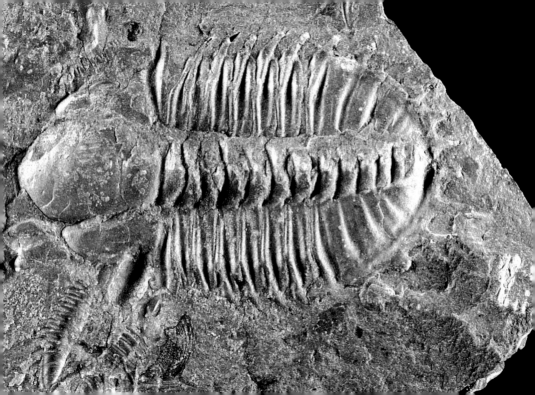

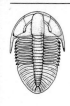

Calymene

Usually found in limestone with fossil brachiopods, corals, and bryozoans, *Calymene* seems to have lived in clear, shallow water. Like most trilobites, it lacked the streamlined shape of a fast-moving predator, and did not have the tools of a predator—limbs with which to catch prey. Not much is known about how trilobites lived, but comparisons with modern crustaceans suggest that they either filtered tiny organisms out of sediment or ate the sediment for its organic content.

Identification 1⅛″ long, ⅝″ wide. Body widest at head and tapering towards tail, with 13 segments. Head semicircular; central region high with 3 pairs of broad lobes at sides. Eyes small. Short tail somewhat triangular.

Age Early Silurian to Middle Devonian.

Range Widespread in North America.

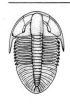

Elrathia

A very common trilobite, *Elrathia* is available in rock shops and souvenir stands everywhere and often made into jewelry. It is not uncommon to find a slab with many specimens of *Elrathia* of various sizes, each representing a different growth stage. Like lobsters, trilobites had to shed their old external skeleton and grow a new one as the body became larger. They went through three major growth stages, and during each one there were changes in body details. Because of these changes, their relative age can easily be determined.

Identification 1″ long, ⅝″ wide. Skeleton oval, with 12–17 body segments. Head larger than body; central region raised, but not reaching outer margin. Short spines at sides of head in the rear. Tail small.

Age Middle Cambrian.

Range Widespread in the western United States.

Dalmanites

A distinctive feature of *Dalmanites* is the long spine on the tail. It has been suggested that this spine was used to stir up sediment for food. But it is unlikely that *Dalmanites* ate moving food, because none of its appendages could be used to capture prey. Another explanation is that *Dalmanites* was a bottom-dweller and its spines supported it on the soft sea floor.

Identification 2¾" long, 1⅝" wide. Skeleton oval, with 12 body segments. Head with flat margin and long, thick spines; central part high, with 3 pairs of distinct furrows. Eyes large and kidney-shaped, with distinct lenses on outer surfaces. Tail with 11–14 segments ending in long spine.

Age Silurian.

Range Eastern and central North America.

Olenellus

Trilobites were among the earliest fossils with hard skeletons. They were the dominant form of life at the beginning of the Cambrian Period, and *Olenellus* is typical of the group. Trilobite eyes were compound like those of modern crustaceans and insects, but the eyes of these earliest trilobites are not well known because they were built in such a way that the visual surface dropped away and was lost during molting or after death.

Identification 3″ long, 2¼″ wide. Skeleton oval, with 18–44 or more body segments, some ending as spines. Head broad and semicircular, with short, strong spines extending from sides; raised central part long, almost cylindrical, with 3 pairs of furrows. Eyes large and concentric. Tail tiny.

Age Early Cambrian.

Range Widespread in North America.

Encrinurus

The most noticeable feature in *Encrinurus* is the bumps on its head. Many trilobites have such bumps, and when they are examined microscopically some of them have hollow spaces just below the surface, while others have a canal that extends to the inner surface of the skeleton. Although their purpose is still unknown, many scientists believe the bumps had a sensory function. Another interesting feature of *Encrinurus* is that when it rolled up, it formed an almost perfect sphere, completely enclosing its underside.

Identification   ¾″ long, 1″ wide. Body with 11–12 segments. Head a little larger than tail; central part large and bulbous, wider at front, and covered with numerous bumps. Eyes small, on short stalks. Tail triangular.

Age   Middle Ordovician to Silurian.

Range   Widespread in North America.

Eurypterus

Extinct relatives of modern horseshoe crabs, eurypterids probably lived in much the same way. They are also related to spiders and scorpions, and more distantly to lobsters, crabs, and trilobites. Although abundant only in New York State, they are found in numerous museums and are illustrated in virtually every book about fossils. In 1984 *Eurypterus* was selected as the official fossil of New York State.

Identification 5½" long, 1½" wide. External skeleton with broad head, compound eyes, 12 movable body segments, and pointed tail. Six pairs of appendages, the first for grasping, the last for balancing or swimming, and the rest for walking.

Age Early Ordovician to Middle Permian.

Range Rarely in Wisconsin, Illinois, Indiana, Ohio, and Pennsylvania. Locally abundant in New York.

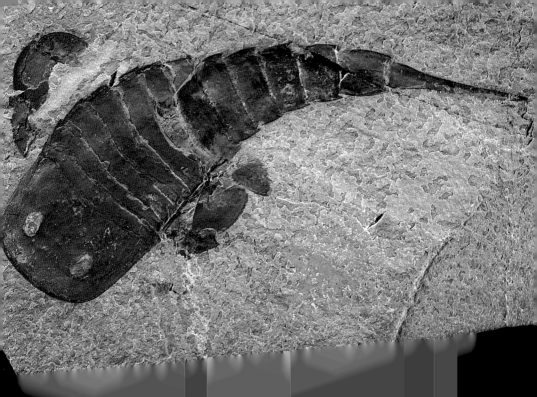

Tetragraptus

Graptolites are commonly found as carbon impressions in black shales, where they are most abundant. Because *Tetragraptus* and many other graptolites were floating animals, when they died they sank into deep, oxygen-poor water and were preserved in the fine sediments on the sea floor. Without oxygen, decay took place slowly, so there was time for the animals to be buried. They are used for dating and correlating rocks in different regions, because they evolved rapidly, and each species existed only briefly and had a wide geographic range due to their floating habits.

Identification	2″ long, ⅟₅₀″ wide. A colony composed of 4 branches connected by threads; each branch with single row of simple, overlapping chambers.
Age	Early Ordovician.
Range	Widespread in North America.

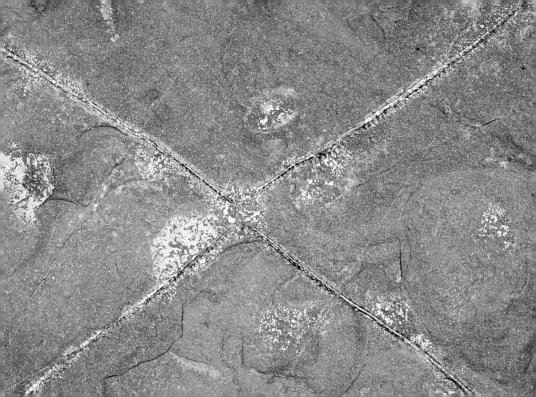

Monograptus

Like most other graptolites, *Monograptus* is usually preserved as a carbon film that often looks like tiny saws scattered over the surface of the rock. When light hits the fossils at just the right angle, they take on a silvery sheen. In fact, a good way to look for them is to rotate the rock, looking for the telltale flash of light. Recent studies of this fossil suggest a close relationship to the pterobranchs—colonial creatures thought to be distantly related to vertebrates.

Identification   1″ long, ⅟₃₂″ wide. A colony arranged in a single row, usually straight, but sometimes curved or coiled. Body chambers cylindrical, conical, or flattened tubes. Position of chambers variable, sometimes separate, touching, or overlapping.

Age   Early Silurian to Early Devonian.

Range   Widespread in North America.

Glossary

Aperture
In gastropods, cephalopods, and bryozoans, the opening through which the animal protrudes.

Appendage
One of several paired, leglike structures on trilobites, *Eurypterus*, insects, and related creatures, used for walking, obtaining food, or other functions.

Axis
In bryozoans, the central stalk of a coiled colony. In gastropods and some cephalopods, an imaginary straight line around which the coils of the shell turn.

Beak
In bivalve mollusks and brachiopods, a pointed area where the two valves come together.

Cast
A replica of a fossil formed when sediment fills the inside of a mold and then hardens.

Cilium
A tiny, hairlike projection that beats rhythmically and, coordinated with others, creates a current that flows over or past an animal. (Plural, cilia)

184

Colonial
Living in colonies, as do some corals and some bryozoans.

Corallite
An individual coral animal in a colonial coral.

Crossbar
In corals and bryozoans, a small link between branches of
a colony or between partitions in a corallite.

Eon
The largest division of geological time; there are two
eons, the Precambrian and Phanerozoic.

Epoch
The shortest division of geological time used in this guide;
a division of a period.

Era
A major division of geological time, shorter than an eon
but longer than a period. The Phanerozoic Eon is divided
into the Paleozoic, Mesozoic, and Cenozoic eras.

Filter feeder
An animal that feeds by straining or filtering tiny
particles out of a current of water.

Igneous rock
Rock that was formerly molten; never contains fossils.

Lophophore
In brachiopods, an organ for feeding and breathing, formed by a pair of grooved arms or lobes on the inside of the upper valve.

Metamorphic rock
Rock that has been altered by pressure and heat deep within the earth's crust. Fossils seldom found here.

Mold
A cavity formed in sediment when a fossil is dissolved by water. The inside cavity bears its impression.

Partition
In corals, one of several thin plates that extend from the outer edge in toward the center.

Period
A division of geological time shorter than an era and longer than an epoch.

Platform
In some corals, a horizontal shelf extending across the cavity occupied by an individual coral animal.

Rhomboid
Having four sides, with opposite sides parallel and adjacent sides unequal in length; seen on bryozoans.

Sedimentary rock
Layered rock that has been formed by the deposition of lime, silt, clay, or sand. Fossils often found here.

Siphuncle
In some cephalopods, a slender tube that runs through each of the shell chambers; often not preserved.

Spicule
In sponges, a tiny, often needlelike structure that interlocks with others to form a skeleton.

Spire
In gastropods, all shell coils except the outermost.

Suture
In chambered cephalopods, a line on the shell marking where the chamber walls attach to the shell inside.

Valve
In bivalve mollusks, one of two platelike shells, one on either side of the body. In brachiopods, one of two plates surrounding the animal, one above and one below.

Index

Credits

Photographs
All photographs were taken by
Townsend P. Dickinson, with
permission of the Museum of
Pennsylvania State University, the
Peabody Museum of Yale University,
Princeton University Museum, and
the Smithsonian Institution,
Washington, D.C.

Cover Photograph
Alethopteris by Townsend P.
Dickinson

Illustrations
Drawings by Dolores R. Santoliquido
and Edward Lam

Chanticleer Staff
Publisher: Paul Steiner
Editor-in-Chief: Gudrun Buettner
Executive Editor: Susan Costello
Managing Editor: Jane Opper
Natural Science Editor: John Farrand, Jr.
Assistant Editor: Amy Hughes
Production Manager: Helga Lose
Production: Gina Stead-Thomas, Helen L.A. Brown
Art Director: Carol Nehring
Art Associates: Ayn Svoboda, Cheryl Miller
Picture Library: Edward Douglas
Design: Massimo Vignelli

The Audubon Society

The National Audubon Society is among the oldest and largest private conservation organizations in the world. With over 560,000 members and more than 500 local chapters across the country, the Society works in behalf of our natural heritage through environmental education and conservation action. It protects wildlife in more than seventy sanctuaries from coast to coast. It also operates outdoor education centers and ecology workshops and publishes the prizewinning AUDUBON magazine, AMERICAN BIRDS magazine, newsletters, films, and other educational materials. For further information regarding membership in the Society, write to the National Audubon Society, 950 Third Avenue, New York, New York 10022.